transformed

Becoming like God's Son
Derek Tidball

BIBLE STUDY RESOURCES FOR
INDIVIDUALS OR SMALL GROUPS

Keswick
Resources

INTER-VARSITY PRESS
36 Causton Street, London SW1P 4ST, England
Email: ivp@ivpbooks.com
Website: www.ivpbooks.com

First published 2016

British Library Cataloguing-in-Publication Data
A catalogue record for this book is available from the British Library.

ISBN: 978–1–78359–454–2
eBook ISBN: 978–1–78359–455–9

Set in Warnock
Typeset in Great Britain by CRB Associates, Potterhanworth, Lincolnshire
Printed and bound in Great Britain by 4edge Limited

*Inter-Varsity Press publishes Christian books that are true to the Bible and that
communicate the gospel, develop discipleship and strengthen the church for its mission
in the world.*

*IVP originated within the Inter-Varsity Fellowship, now the Universities and Colleges
Christian Fellowship, a student movement connecting Christian Unions in universities and
colleges throughout Great Britain, and a member movement of the International Fellowship
of Evangelical Students. Website: www.uccf.org.uk. That historic association is maintained,
and all senior IVP staff and committee members subscribe to the UCCF Basis of Faith.*

I'm happy to commend this study guide, which will be of benefit to both individuals and small groups. It is packed with challenging biblical insights.
James Collins, Senior Minister, Purley Baptist Church

Seeing Jesus afresh through the lens of this guide will stir your heart, open your mind, engage your imagination, and grow your desire to be like Christ in the whole of life. Far from 'other-worldly', this study guide maps out some vital pathways for followers of Jesus through the gritty reality of everyday contexts and relationships. Yes, the terrain is challenging. But this is a grace-filled, Christ-dependent journey to become more like Jesus. Come join!
Tracy Cotterell, Managing Director, LICC

Becoming like Jesus is central to God's agenda for every disciple, so don't read and engage with these studies unless you are ready and willing to change! Practical, thoughtful and designed for group learning, they will challenge you to reflect and act on what imitating Jesus looks like in your life and context.
Patrick Mitchel, Principal, Belfast Bible College

This set of study notes from Derek Tidball would make a very useful course for church discipleship groups or home-study groups. In challenging readers to grow more fully into the image of Christ, the studies do not default on practical application or suggestions for deeper reflection, and they also indicate the rich Old Testament background to Jesus' ministry where appropriate. The explanatory notes at the back will be a great help to group discussion.
Sally Nelson, Tutor, St Barnabas Theological Centre, Sheffield

This study guide provides some very interesting material to work through either in your own personal study time or as a small group. It examines what it really means to become like Jesus from a biblical perspective, and also applies this in practice. I really liked the way it is divided into different sections and also the encouragement for further reading. This is a down-to-earth study guide that is highly recommended.
Sharon Prior, Senior Tutor at Moorlands College

With profound insights, helpful application and humour, Derek's study guide takes us right to the heart of what it means to follow Jesus. If we are willing, the truths contained here will get under our skin and transform us further into his likeness.
Nick Sharp, Pastor, Grace Church Nottingham

This study guide brings together Derek's outstanding biblical understanding and his grounding in the real world to produce a fantastic resource that I am sure will be both enjoyable and fruitful for all who engage with it.
Rich Webb, Senior Pastor of Upton Vale Baptist Church and Moderator of the Baptist Union Board of Trustees

Derek has once again opened the Scriptures to help us see Jesus afresh. The format moves from study, through prayer, to action, so that the individual or group is open to the character of Jesus being formed in them. I have been reading this book on my way to a retreat and know it will prove useful.
Paul Wilson, Development Worker, Methodist Evangelicals Together

Contents

Introduction

Every Christian who thinks about it would say that they want to be like Jesus. None would vote against that, especially if they have been fired up recently by going to a Bible conference or have listened to an inspirational and motivational preacher. But what does it mean to be like Jesus?

The ambition is admirable, but does it mean that we need to wear sandals, speak Aramaic, ride donkeys and grow beards or be circumcised (if we're male, that is)? Does it mean that we should be able to walk on water, feed the world's hungry at a stroke or should never own a home? Some have thought so!

Silly answers like this are easily dismissed. We recognize that there are some things that Jesus did uniquely as Creator and Saviour of the world, which we are not called upon to reproduce in our lives. We also recognize that we live in a different world from the one Jesus inhabited, so we have no difficulty in wearing shoes, speaking English and driving cars, and we are thankful for the advances of science and technology. But these differences just highlight the problem. Our world is so very different from that of Jesus' day, so it makes us ask whether a simple call to be like Jesus isn't too simplistic to guide and shape our lives.

How does it help when

- we're faced with recalcitrant teenage children?
- we're negotiating with the boss about a fair wage?
- we face difficult ethical medical decisions?
- we're confronted with some very messed-up lives?
- we're made to feel like relics in a world that has consigned traditional sexual ethics to the scrap heap?
- we're overwhelmed by the barrage of news about global violence, migration and poverty?
- we're expected to know exactly what we should do about climate change?
- we're dealing with other issues the media decides to put on our agenda?

Taking a seminar on 'Growing Deeper with God' some time ago, an experienced pastor confessed, 'The more I go on in ministry, the less clear I am about what it means to be like Jesus.' Don't be too hard on him. He was at the sharp end, dealing every day with people living in damaging social environments who brought their broken lives to him looking for instant answers that didn't seem to come.

So when we say we want to be like Jesus, what do we mean in our day and age?

These studies are designed to take us back to basics and discover something more about what the New Testament call to be like Jesus means. They don't give detailed guidance about parenting, employment issues or international migration, because that's not the approach the New Testament writers took. Rather, they challenge us to become particular types of people, and educate us about the sort of person God wants us to be. Then, as people reborn in his image, we have the responsibility, and the assistance of the Holy Spirit, to work things through so that we live transformed, like Jesus, in our very different world.

SESSION 1

Transformed: becoming like God's Son **in godliness**

▶ GETTING STARTED

From an early age we learn to imitate those we admire. Often we're not even conscious of doing so, as when children imitate their parents, but sometimes we do consciously learn to imitate others we admire. Many a child practises the dance steps or guitar moves of their celebrity heroes and demands to dress like them or adopt their hairstyles. Even mature preachers have been known to imitate the accent, repeat key phrases or adopt the gestures of preachers they think of highly.

How does this becoming like others happen? Children become like their parents because they live with them and see them day in and day out in all sorts of different situations. Fans may only relate to their idols at a distance. Nevertheless, they become like their heroes by spending as much time as possible listening to them, watching them, attending their gigs and buying their music. The unsurprising secret of becoming like our ideal models is having as close a relationship with them as possible and spending as much time as we can with them.

Becoming like Jesus is the same. To be like Jesus requires us not just to brush with him occasionally, but to steadily, surely 'remain' in him.

READ *John 15:1–17*

I am the true vine, and my Father is the gardener. He cuts off every branch in me that bears no fruit, while every branch that does bear fruit he prunes so that it will be even more fruitful. You are already clean because of the word I have spoken to you. Remain in me, as I also remain in you. No branch can bear fruit by itself; it must remain in the vine. Neither can you bear fruit unless you remain in me.

I am the vine; you are the branches. If you remain in me and I in you, you will bear much fruit; apart from me you can do nothing. If you do not remain in me, you are like a branch that is thrown away and withers; such branches are picked up, thrown into the fire and burned. If you remain in me and my words remain in you, ask whatever you wish, and it will be done for you. This is to my Father's glory, that you bear much fruit, showing yourselves to be my disciples.

As the Father has loved me, so have I loved you. Now remain in my love. If you keep my commands, you will remain in my love, just as I have kept my Father's commands and remain in his love. I have told you this so that my joy may be in you and that your joy may be complete. My command is this: love each other as I have loved you. Greater love has no one than this: to lay down one's life for one's friends. You are my friends if you do what I command. I no longer call you servants, because a servant does not know his master's business. Instead, I have called you friends, for everything that I learned from my Father I have made known to you. You did not choose me, but I chose you and appointed you so that you might go and bear fruit – fruit that will last – and so that whatever you ask in my name the Father will give you. This is my command: love each other.

FOCUS ON THE THEME

1. Share stories – serious or humorous – of ways in which you or your children imitate those they admire, like teachers, athletes, rock stars or preachers. How do they learn to be like them? What does this suggest about our wanting to be like Jesus?

 # WHAT DOES THE BIBLE SAY?

2. How does the image of the vine help us to understand what it means to 'remain' in Jesus?

3. Jesus mentions his word or commands (verses 7, 10, 17) and his love (verse 9). How do they help us to remain in him?

4. Note the importance of bearing 'fruit' (verses 2, 4, 5, 8, 16). What does Jesus mean by fruit, and why fruit that 'will last' (verse 16)? Jesus explains fruit in terms of discipleship in verse 8.

Fruit-bearing for God is not a human possibility; it is Christ's work through us. The alternatives are starkly expressed; separate from Christ, 'no fruit'; united to Christ, 'much fruit' (v. 5). A continual dependence upon a living Saviour, 'communing' with him through the Holy Spirit, and submission to him in all things – these are the characteristics of a life in which God is glorified through the bearing of fruit to his praise.

(Bruce Milne, *The Message of John*, p. 221)

◎ GOING DEEPER

5. The secret of abundant fruit-bearing lies in wise, if painful, pruning (verse 2) at the hands of the Master Gardener. In what ways have you known God to wield the pruning knife in your life?

Even if we are bearing fruit, there is no ground for contentment; there is still need for the pruning knife of the husbandman ... That cleansing may be painful. It is almost bound to be. But the pain can be the condition of more abundant fruit.

(William Temple, *Readings in St John's Gospel*, p. 247)

6. How do you react to Jesus' words in verse 6? Who do you think Jesus had in mind when he uttered this warning?

7. Jesus' relationship with his Father is the pattern for our relationship with him. What, according to verse 10, characterizes that relationship? How does John 5:16–30 supplement the picture of their relationship?

 **LIVING IT OUT**

8.   What habits can I adopt to enable Jesus' words, 'remain in me', to become more of a reality? Would the discipline of more regular Bible reading, intentional Bible study or memorizing Bible verses assist? Take steps to put your conclusion into practical action.

9.   The secret of answered prayer (verse 7) is that our prayers are shaped by, and based on, God's own words. Review the way you pray individually and together. Do we need to change our way of praying so that our prayers are not a list of 'I wants', but are consciously based on the character, promises and commands of God? The way Nehemiah prays in Nehemiah 1:4–11, or Paul's prayers for the churches of Philippi, Ephesus and Colossae may prove a helpful guide.

10.   Farmers are never vague about the fruitfulness of their harvests. Yet many Christians and churches are content to be vague about the spiritual harvest, or duck the question altogether. Do your accounts. Take stock. When did you last produce a harvest for Jesus? If it's some time since, is it possibly because you are no longer remaining in him?

▲ PRAYER TIME

Find out about places around the world where abundant spiritual harvests are presently being reaped for Christ, and begin by thanking God for them.

Pray for an increased harvest in the United Kingdom.

Pray for increased fruit-bearing in your own life and church.

● FURTHER STUDY

Jesus didn't pluck this image of the vine and the branches out of the air. Israel was portrayed as a vine (Isaiah 5:1–7) that had been carefully tended and protected, but 'it yielded only bad fruit'.

Isaiah 5:7 tells us that the fruit God was looking for was 'justice' and 'righteousness', or right living. How does that impact our understanding of fruit-bearing in John 15?

In Isaiah, God painfully asks what more he could have done than he had already. In the end God determines to destroy the vineyard and turn it into a wasteland.

How much did Jesus have Israel in mind when he spoke about branches being 'picked up, thrown into the fire and burned' (John 15:6)? How might Paul's adaptation of the picture of the branches in Romans 11:11–25 affect our understanding of Jesus' words?

By way of conclusion, look up the same picture in Psalm 80:8–16. Note the urgent request repeated three times: 'Restore us, O God' (verses 3, 7, 19). Is this what we should be praying today?

Transformed: becoming like God's Son **in character**

▶ GETTING STARTED

We know nothing of Jesus' personality or even his appearance. We don't know if he was tall or short, whether he was slim or swarthy, had a beard or not, was humorous or even how extrovert he was, although we can make some intelligent guesses about some of these.

Appearance and personality matter greatly in our contemporary society, as the cult of the celebrity shows. But they were of little importance until recently. Previous generations were more concerned about character – the moral qualities, both good and bad, both virtues and vices, which went to make up a person. Character was what mattered.

We can tell a lot about the character of Jesus from the Gospels. We know of his compassion, especially for the underdog, his patience with his disciples, his opposition to hypocrisy and false religion, his commitment to truth and his passion for God's grace and righteousness to be made known. People spoke of him as 'good' and 'a man of integrity'. They took his claims of closeness to God seriously because his life made them believable. They knew they'd never catch him out, so they were forced to resort to ridicule, harassment and even outright lying to defame him.

Being like Christ means we will work at imitating his character in our own lives.

READ *Colossians 3:1-17*

Since, then, you have been raised with Christ, set your hearts on things above, where Christ is, seated at the right hand of God. Set your minds on things above, not on earthly things. For you died, and your life is now hidden with Christ in God. When Christ, who is your life, appears, then you also will appear with him in glory.

Put to death, therefore, whatever belongs to your earthly nature: sexual immorality, impurity, lust, evil desires and greed, which is idolatry. Because of these, the wrath of God is coming. You used to walk in these ways, in the life you once lived. But now you must also rid yourselves of all such things as these: anger, rage, malice, slander, and filthy language from your lips. Do not lie to each other, since you have taken off your old self with its practices and have put on the new self, which is being renewed in knowledge in the image of its Creator. Here there is no Gentile or Jew, circumcised or uncircumcised, barbarian, Scythian, slave or free, but Christ is all, and is in all.

Therefore, as God's chosen people, holy and dearly loved, clothe yourselves with compassion, kindness, humility, gentleness and patience. Bear with each other and forgive one another if any of you has a grievance against someone. Forgive as the Lord forgave you. And over all these virtues put on love, which binds them all together in perfect unity.

Let the peace of Christ rule in your hearts, since as members of one body you were called to peace. And be thankful. Let the message of Christ dwell among you richly as you teach and admonish one another with all wisdom through psalms, hymns, and songs from the Spirit, singing to God with gratitude in your hearts. And whatever you do, whether in word or deed, do it all in the name of the Lord Jesus, giving thanks to God the Father through him.

FOCUS ON THE THEME

1. Think about people you know well, like work colleagues, relatives, members of your church or of a club to which you belong. Whom do you admire? What makes them attractive to you? Are they godly characteristics? What aspects of their character do you least like, and why?

WHAT DOES THE BIBLE SAY?

2. What do verses 1–5 tell us are the steps we can take to Christlike living? Give consideration to all the instructions Paul mentions here, including what it means in practice to 'put to death ... whatever belongs to [our] earthly nature'.

Paul was here describing the process of mortification, the daily putting to death of the flesh through the disciplines of prayer, fasting, repentance, and self-control.

(Timothy George, *Galatians*, p. 405)

3. How does this passage, climaxing with verse 11, emphasize that a Christlike character is about relationships rather than merely individual traits?

4. What clues are given in verses 16–17 as to how we can nurture a Christlike character?

◎ GOING DEEPER

5. Paul often speaks of the way we *will be* raised with Christ at the resurrection (for example, Romans 6:4–5). Here he says, 'you *have been* raised with Christ'. How does this give reassurance to the diffident believers in Colossae?

6. The imagery of the Christian's wardrobe runs through verses 12–14 ('clothe yourselves'; 'put on love'). Look at Romans 13:14 and Galatians 3:27 where Paul also speaks of being clothed with Christ. What items do these verses suggest should be found in the Christian's wardrobe?

7. The vision of verse 10 is the renewal of God's image in us. We were made in his image (Genesis 1:27), but the image was corrupted through sin. Who, according to Colossians 1:15 and Hebrews 1:3, is the perfect image of God? How does that help us to understand what God's image in us should look like?

 **LIVING IT OUT**

8. How far do I compartmentalize my church life from the other aspects of my life, such as my work, family or leisure? Do I keep God confined to church? What would people say about my character at work or in the family (see verse 17)?

9. According to verse 11, what place does racism have in the church? Does your church reflect the multi-ethnic nature of the UK? If not, how can you contact and embrace Christian brothers and sisters from other ethnic groups?

Purely private atonement is at odds with the biblical vision of individuals who are saved into community. Salvation involves personal transformation, of course, but it doesn't stop there. The gospel of the kingdom creates disciples with public commitments.

(Jim Wallis, *On God's Side*, p. 14)

10. Colossians repeatedly stresses the need for thankfulness, as here in verses 16–17. Gratitude is perhaps a forgotten ingredient in character formation. List those things for which you thank God today, and keep them in front of you.

PRAYER TIME

Use Paul's list of 'the fruit of the Spirit' in Galatians 5:22–23 as the basis of reflective prayer. Read through the qualities slowly, pausing over each one. Ask, 'Is this a quality I possess in plenty, or do I need to cultivate it further, or have I not yet begun to exercise it?'

Some qualities seem to be in tension with others: the faithful person may not exhibit forbearance towards those who are less reliable, and the self-controlled person may not find gentleness easy with those who aren't self-disciplined. So it's unlikely you'll score well on every quality.

Then pray specifically for the Spirit's help to protect your strong qualities and in developing those characteristics that are weak at present. Ask God for guidance as to what steps you can take to bear better quality fruit of all kinds.

FURTHER STUDY

Read through some other passages that set out the Christian's character: Romans 12:3–21; 1 Corinthians 13; Galatians 5:16–26; Ephesians 4:17 – 5:21; 2 Peter 1:5–9; 1 John 3:16–18. What composite picture do they draw of the Christian life?

SESSION 3

Transformed: becoming like God's Son **in serving**

▶ GETTING STARTED

When you go to a restaurant, how much attention do you pay to the waiter, or do you take them for granted? After all, they're there to serve you: that's their job. Now imagine yourself in the company of a powerful person — a celebrity, politician or wealthy industrialist. Do you treat them the same way as you did the waiter? Most of us foolishly think that the powerful are more interesting, important and influential than those who serve. Jesus tells us that this is not so in God's kingdom, and to be like him means much more than treating servants as human beings. It means actually becoming servants ourselves.

READ *John 13:1-5, 12-17*

It was just before the Passover Festival. Jesus knew that the hour had come for him to leave this world and go to the Father. Having loved his own who were in the world, he loved them to the end.

The evening meal was in progress, and the devil had already prompted Judas, the son of Simon Iscariot, to betray Jesus. Jesus knew that the Father had put all things under his power, and that he had come from God and was returning to God; so he got up from the meal, took off his outer clothing, and wrapped a towel around his waist. After that, he poured water into a basin and began to wash his disciples' feet, drying them with the towel that was wrapped around him . . .

When he had finished washing their feet, he put on his clothes and returned to his place. 'Do you understand what I have done for you?' he asked them. 'You call me "Teacher" and "Lord", and rightly so, for that is what I am. Now that I, your Lord and Teacher, have washed your feet, you also should wash one another's feet. I have set you an example that you should do as I have done for you. Very truly I tell you, no servant is greater than his master, nor is a messenger greater than the one who sent him. Now that you know these things, you will be blessed if you do them.

FOCUS ON THE THEME

1. The successful TV series *Downton Abbey* portrayed a world sharply divided between the servants downstairs and the powerful upstairs, as in many ways the world still is. Which role would you most like to have played and why?

WHAT DOES THE BIBLE SAY?

2. What does John tell us about the circumstances of the meal when Jesus washed his disciples' feet (verses 1–4)? Why might Jesus have been legitimately distracted?

3. In what ways does this particular action of washing feet represent the whole of Jesus' approach to his incarnation and mission?

4. Jesus explains several reasons why we should 'do as I have done for you' (verse 15). What are they? In the light of them, why is it so hard to act aside our egos and act as he did?

GOING DEEPER

5. Isaiah wrote several songs about 'the servant' (42:1–4; 49:1–6; 50:4–9; 52:13 – 53:12). What characteristics of the servant of Isaiah 42:1–4 (Spirit-filled, passion for justice, gentleness. faithfulness) can you identify in the ministry of Jesus? Share some of the stories of his ministry together and then look at Mark 10:45 by way of a summary.

6.   Why might John 13 be seen as a dramatic portrayal enacting what Paul said of Jesus in Philippians 2:5–11? What do these passages have in common?

7.   What does Mark 10:35–45 teach us about the practice of Christian leadership?

Jesus gave us a new norm of greatness. If you want to be important – wonderful. If you want to be recognized – wonderful. If you want to be great – wonderful. But recognize that he who is greatest among you shall be your servant. That's a new definition of greatness. And this morning, the thing that I like about it: by giving that definition of greatness, it means that everybody can be great, because everybody can serve.

(Martin Luther King, 'The Drum Major Instinct', a sermon delivered on 4 February 1968)

♥ LIVING IT OUT

8.   Check your attitudes. Are you the first to serve, or do you delight in being served? Would others agree with your verdict?

9.   What is the contemporary equivalent of foot washing? Cleaning cars, cooking meals, tending gardens, giving lifts? List a few people whose feet you can wash.

A Salvation Army Cadet, Samuel Logan Brengle, was rebelling at cleaning his fellow cadet's shoes when he saw a picture: Jesus was the central figure and he was washing his disciples' feet! His Lord, who had come from . . . the glories of heaven and the adoration of its hosts bending over the feet of uncouth, unlearned fishermen, washing them and humbling himself, taking the form of a servant! Brengle's heart was brought low. 'Dear Lord,' he whispered, 'thou did'st wash their feet; I will black their boots.'

(Quoted in John Stott, *The Incomparable Christ*, p. 146)

10. What steps can be taken to make leadership in your church – leadership at every level, not just the minister! – more like that of a servant and less like a powerful boss?

▲ PRAYER TIME

'In every situation, by prayer and petition, with thanksgiving, present your requests to God' (Philippians 4:6).

First, give thanks for those who have served us in life, naming parents, family, teachers, mentors, church leaders and a host of others.

Second, pray for the Spirit's help in putting to death our egos so that we are free to serve others. Confess particular situations to God in prayer where the temptation to assert self is strong. Pray that we might increasingly become like Christ in his humility

 **FURTHER STUDY**

A good life, according to James, is one where there is evidence of 'deeds done in the humility that comes from wisdom' (James 3:13). He then outlines two kinds of wisdom: one that is 'earthly, unspiritual, demonic'; the other that is 'wisdom that comes from heaven' (James 3:14–18). Look through the contrasts and apply them to the world around you. How different our world would be if people lived by 'the wisdom of heaven'. Cultivate that wisdom for your own life, starting by admitting your need for help.

SESSION 4

Transformed: becoming like God's Son **in compassion**

▶ GETTING STARTED

Day after day our news media makes us conscious that we live in a world of desperate need. One day the headlines are about a city destroyed by war, the next it's a community devastated by a hurricane or floods. We hear of millions facing starvation because their crops have failed, mayhem and death caused by terrorism, a village buried in a mudslide with great loss of life, or a whole region devastated by earthquake. At the time of writing, the news headlines have been dominated for months by the plight of migrants fleeing across hundreds of miles to the safety of Europe from their war-torn, poverty-stricken and politically unstable home countries.

The problems and needs seem immense and unsolvable. Like Paul, in a different context, we want to cry, 'Who is equal to such a task?' (2 Corinthians 2:16). No wonder the charities and emergency appeals that strive to relieve suffering fear that the public may stop giving because of compassion fatigue.

Jesus was deeply moved by suffering and need. Although he tired, as any human being does, he never suffered from compassion fatigue. Being like him means that we too should be people of compassion.

READ *Mark 6:30–44*

The apostles gathered round Jesus and reported to him all they had done and taught. Then, because so many people were coming and going that they did not even have a chance to eat, he said to them, 'Come with me by yourselves to a quiet place and get some rest.'

So they went away by themselves in a boat to a solitary place. But many who saw them leaving recognized them and ran on foot from all the towns and got there ahead of them. When Jesus landed and saw a large crowd, he had compassion on them, because they were like sheep without a shepherd. So he began teaching them many things.

By this time it was late in the day, so his disciples came to him. 'This is a remote place,' they said, 'and it's already very late. Send the people away so that they can go to the surrounding countryside and villages and buy themselves something to eat.'

But he answered, 'You give them something to eat.'

They said to him, 'That would take more than half a year's wages! Are we to go and spend that much on bread and give it to them to eat?'

'How many loaves do you have?' he asked. 'Go and see.'

When they found out, they said, 'Five – and two fish.'

Then Jesus directed them to make all the people sit down in groups on the green grass. So they sat down in groups of hundreds and fifties. Taking the five loaves and the two fish and looking up to heaven, he gave thanks and broke the loaves. Then he gave them to his disciples to distribute to the people. He also divided the two fish among them all. They all ate and were satisfied, and the disciples picked up twelve basketfuls of broken pieces of bread and fish. The number of the men who had eaten was five thousand.

FOCUS ON THE THEME

1. When confronted with yet another urgent appeal to help people
    in need, what is our reaction? Are we deeply affected by it? Do we
    manage our compassion by dealing with the need at arm's length?
    Or do we, in all honesty, suffer from compassion fatigue?

WHAT DOES THE BIBLE SAY?

2. The desire of Jesus and his disciples for some rest seems to have
    been thwarted by the crowds that constantly followed them.
    How did he react in spite of his weariness? Did the disciples react
    in the same way?

3. Jesus describes the 'large crowd' as 'like sheep without a shepherd'.
    What does this picture convey to you? Do you identify with the
    disciples in verses 35–37? What steps did Jesus take in feeding
    a large crowd (see verses 38–40). This is not the only time
    he performed a mass miracle (see Mark 8:1–13 and Luke
    17:11–19).

Dick France explains that the Greek word for compassion is a 'strongly emotional' word: *'No single English term does justice to it: compassion, pity, sympathy and fellow feeling all convey part of it, but "his heart went out" perhaps presents more fully the emotional force of the underlying metaphor of "gut response".'* Wherever it is used, France says, *'there is not only sympathy with a person's need, but also a practical response which meets that need . . . It . . . describes the Jesus of the Gospel stories in a nutshell.'*

(R. T. France, *The Gospel of Matthew*, p. 373)

4. After teaching them, Christ's compassion expressed itself in feeding the hungry. What does the feeding of the 5,000 teach us about God and about Jesus Christ himself?

You can't tell a man about the love of God if he has an empty stomach.

(William Booth, founder of the Salvation Army)

◎ GOING DEEPER

5. The first thing Jesus did when he felt compassion for them was to 'teach them many things' (verse 34). Why was that a compassionate thing to do? How much should it influence our exercise of Christian compassion?

6. Read Matthew 9. What were the various needs of people that provoked Jesus to compassion?

And what were Jesus' responses as a result of his compassion?

See also:

- Matthew 14:14

- Matthew 20:34

7. Look at Exodus 34:6, a fundamental description of the compassionate character of God that is often repeated in the Old Testament. How does that square with his holiness and judgment?

LIVING IT OUT

8. You can't solve the problems of the whole world, but you can start somewhere. If you are not already doing so, can you identify and support

- at least one person who needs practical help?

- a mission or evangelistic agency?

- a relief and development agency working overseas?

9. How do those outside view your church? Is it known as a community of compassion? If not, what initiatives could be taken to enable it to change its culture, and how could you wisely contribute to that change?

10. Review your financial giving. By any standards, Western Christians are among the richest in the world. The giving of a tenth (tithe) is a good starting point, but should never limit us. How much do we give to our local church, to Christian missions and to social needs?

▲ PRAYER TIME

'They all joined together constantly in prayer . . .' (Acts 1:14). Join in praying:

- for those who face desperate situations in their lives
- for those mission and relief agencies seeking to relieve distress
- that those causing distress may repent
- that the UN and world governments may have wisdom in solving global problems
- for righteousness to flourish
- that the church locally may become increasingly a community of compassion
- for softness of heart and a rejection of hard attitudes and judgmentalism
- that God may guide you in your exercise of practical compassion.

 FURTHER STUDY

Look further into the compassion of God, noting in particular that he is compassionate towards:

- his covenant people (2 Kings 13:23; Nehemiah 9:17–28; Hosea 2:19)
- the captive and oppressed (Exodus 3:7–10)
- the weak and vulnerable (Exodus 22:25–27; Deuteronomy 10:18; 24:17–21)
- returning sinners (Deuteronomy 30:1–3; 2 Chronicles 30:9; Jonah 4:2)
- all he has made (Psalm 145:9).

With justice the psalmist claims,

> The LORD is gracious and righteous;
> our God is full of compassion.
> (Psalm 116:5)

SESSION 5

Transformed: becoming like God's Son **in justice**

▶ GETTING STARTED

Jesus met constant hostility from 'the great and the good' because he was 'a friend of tax collectors and sinners' (Luke 7:34). He provoked the ire of the powerful, with vested interests, because, as Luke's Gospel particularly emphasizes, he acted on behalf of those whom society wrote off as unimportant, undeserving or living outside of the boundaries of religious respectability. He did more than befriend them. Time and again he acted to transform their situations through miracles or other acts of mercy.

God is a God of justice, and justice is fundamental to God's kingdom. People suffered because they were not living under God's just reign. Jesus' ministry was one of restoring justice to those who had suffered injustice, whether as a result of Satan's work, unjust human actions or simply as inhabitants of a fallen world. While the language of justice may not be used too much in the gospel, justice is fundamental to the idea of the kingdom of God. And Paul, of course, later develops the idea in terms of justification.

However, Jesus' actions were never merely about improving their lot in this life. He came to call those in need to repentance, to a change of direction in their lives, and to experience God's forgiveness for sin.

One Sabbath morning he set out his mission in the synagogue in his home town by quoting Isaiah 61:1–2. His mission was authentically holistic, blending evangelism and social action in a way that we rarely accomplish today. Becoming like Jesus means we will share his commitment to the vulnerable and marginalized, act on their behalf for justice, and have a passion to lead them to experience the full grace of God in their lives. However, it may also mean that we will provoke the same opposition he did, and we need to be prepared to pay that cost in our bid for Christlikeness.

READ *Luke 4:16–21*

He went to Nazareth, where he had been brought up, and on the Sabbath day he went into the synagogue, as was his custom. He stood up to read, and the scroll of the prophet Isaiah was handed to him. Unrolling it, he found the place where it is written:

'The Spirit of the Lord is on me,
> *because he has anointed me*
> *to proclaim good news to the poor.*
He has sent me to proclaim freedom for the prisoners
> *and recovery of sight for the blind,*
to set the oppressed free,
> *to proclaim the year of the Lord's favour.'*

Then he rolled up the scroll, gave it back to the attendant and sat down. The eyes of everyone in the synagogue were fastened on him. He began by saying to them, 'Today this scripture is fulfilled in your hearing.'

 FOCUS ON THE THEME

1. Who might be considered the equivalent of 'tax collectors and sinners' in our contemporary world?

 WHAT DOES THE BIBLE SAY?

2. What, according to verse 18, is the source of Jesus' power to accomplish his mission?

Evidently Jesus thinks that his ministry is going to produce radical changes in the society of his day, sufficiently important as to interpret them as signs of the coming of a new era of justice – the era of God's reign. The Spirit has anointed him as the one who comes to accomplish God's liberation of the oppressed . . .

(René Padilla, 'The Kingdom of God and the Mission of the Church', p. 76)

3.   What is the meaning of 'proclaim' in verse 18, and what was the good news Jesus proclaimed?

4.   When does Jesus say that Isaiah's prophesy will be fulfilled, and through whom? What implications does this have for our mission activity?

◎ GOING DEEPER

5.   Can we identify whom Jesus particularly had in mind when he mentioned the poor, prisoners, the blind and the oppressed? Who are their equivalents today?

6.   Jesus stops short of quoting the whole of Isaiah 61:2 and omits 'and the day of vengeance of our God'. Why do you think he does this? Is his omission deliberate?

7. 'The year of the Lord's favour' points back to the Jubilee Year, outlined in Leviticus 25, when all debts were written off and people were restored to their homes and properties. What significance does this have for understanding Jesus' ministry?

♥ LIVING IT OUT

8. How can we share in Jesus' mission to 'set the oppressed free'? Share some practical examples.

9. Compare your church's approach to mission to the way Jesus states his mission here. Is it as Christ-centred? Is it as holistic, combining evangelism and social action?

The Christian community is more than a community in which the rich help the poor. It is a community in which broken people saved by grace struggle together to demonstrate to a lost world the liberating reality of Christ's loving rule.

(Tim Chester, 'Walk Humbly with Your God', p. 35)

10. What are the primary community needs around your church? Don't just go on impressions or make assumptions, but ascertain some facts by asking your local authority, councillors or other community leaders. The reality may not be what you had expected, and you might be able to make a difference.

▲ PRAYER TIME

Share with each other the particular needs of the world that concern you. Then intercede for God's grace to be at work in that area, and pray for the agencies working in Christ's name among those in need. These concerns might include:

- the homeless
- those struggling with addiction
- the sufferers of abuse
- people with disabilities, either mental or physical
- displaced persons and migrant populations
- the victims of war
- those subject to political or religious oppression
- populations affected by drought or famine
- those in need of relief, aid and development work.

⬤ FURTHER STUDY

Use the internet to track down a Christian agency working in an area that particularly interests you, and actively take steps to support it.

Many social action charities are expressions of the commitment of local churches to their areas, such as New Hope Trust, Watford (www.newhope.org.uk), which provides food banks and help for the homeless.

Other national agencies might include:

Christian Solidarity Worldwide (working for religious freedom and human rights: www.csw.org.uk)

Home for Good (adoption and fostering agency: www.homeforgood.org.uk)

Prospects (working among those with learning disabilities: www.prospects.org.uk)

Tearfund (relief and development: www.tearfund.org)

The Micah Network (a network of Christian organizations devoted to integral mission: www.micahnetwork.org)

Torch Trust (supporting people with sight loss: www.torchtrust.org)

The Cinnamon Network (enabling local churches to help those most at need in their communities: www.cinnamonnetwork.co.uk)

But the list is endless . . .

SESSION 6

Transformed: becoming like God's Son **in suffering**

▶ GETTING STARTED

Suffering is something most of us try to avoid. We view it as a necessary evil, an inevitable consequence of living in a fallen world. Yet God can turn something negative into something very positive. The biblical picture suggests that suffering, far from being something to resist, or even merely incidental, is an essential instrument in God's hands for reshaping us to conform to his will and become more like Jesus. We already encountered this in Session 1 in our consideration of the pruning God does as we remain in Christ.

This session views suffering through a slightly different lens, as it focuses on Jesus' teaching about his disciples taking up their cross. The crucifixion of Jesus was the greatest event in history, and without his undergoing this brutal execution, he could not have accomplished his mission. But the cross is not only a historic event; it is also an enduring pattern and way of life for those who follow Christ – a hallmark of discipleship. Becoming like Jesus inevitably involves his disciples uniting with him in suffering.

READ *Mark 8:31-38*

He then began to teach them that the Son of Man must suffer many things and be rejected by the elders, the chief priests and the teachers of the law, and that he must be killed and after three days rise again. He spoke plainly about this, and Peter took him aside and began to rebuke him.

But when Jesus turned and looked at his disciples, he rebuked Peter. 'Get behind me, Satan!' he said. 'You do not have in mind the concerns of God, but merely human concerns.'

Then he called the crowd to him along with his disciples and said: 'Whoever wants to be my disciple must deny themselves and take up their cross and follow me. For whoever wants to save their life will lose it, but whoever loses their life for me and for the gospel will save it. What good is it for someone to gain the whole world, yet forfeit their soul? Or what can anyone give in exchange for their soul? If anyone is ashamed of me and my words in this adulterous and sinful generation, the Son of Man will be ashamed of them when he comes in his Father's glory with the holy angels.'

 FOCUS ON THE THEME

1. Think back to a particular time of suffering in your own life. What range of feelings and emotions did you experience? How did your suffering impact your view of God?

WHAT DOES THE BIBLE SAY?

2. How does Peter respond to Jesus' announcement about his suffering and death? Why do you think he responded like this?

3. How does Jesus define what it means to take up one's cross in verses 34–35?

We must do something about the cross and one of two things only can we do – flee it or die upon it.

(A. W. Tozer, quoted in Warren W. Wiersbe, *The Best of A. W. Tozer*, p. 135)

4. Give some practical examples of what Jesus meant when he said, 'whoever loses their life for me and for the gospel will save it' (verse 36).

GOING DEEPER

5. In verse 31 Jesus twice uses the word 'must' about his suffering and being killed. Why is there a 'must' about it?

6. Peter's reaction is one with which many would identify, yet Jesus harshly rebukes him and calls him 'Satan' as a result. Explore why Jesus responds like this. Why Satan? And how would you react to such a rebuke?

7. Look up the following passages:

   - Romans 6:1–4

   - Philippians 3:10–11

   Do these verses help in understanding why carrying the cross is not an optional extra for super-disciples, but applies to 'whoever wants to be my disciple'?

Knowing Christ involves sharing in his sufferings – and is a cause for constant joy, not because suffering is enjoyable but because it is evidence of [our] intimate relationship with [the] Lord . . . Christian life is cruciform in character; God's people, even as they live presently through the power of Christ's resurrection, are as their Lord forever marked by the cross.

(Gordon Fee, *Philippians*, pp. 149–150)

 **LIVING IT OUT**

8. Jesus' teaching is the exact opposite of conventional cultural values that assert 'my rights' and the expectation of a self-centred life if we are to live it to the full. How can we encourage one another to live counter-culturally, according to the spiritual principle Jesus taught?

9. Jesus calls his disciples to some very decisive action: 'deny', 'take up'. What actions am I going to take to obey his teaching?

He is no fool who gives what he cannot keep to gain that which he cannot lose.

(Jim Elliot, Journal entry, 28 October 1949.
Elliot, a missionary to Ecuador, was martyred in 1956.)

10. Reflect on your church's teaching and collective lifestyle. How much does it conform to Jesus' radical teaching, or how much does it endorse conventional values, albeit in the guise of suburban niceness?

▲ PRAYER TIME

A prayer from Matthew Henry's *A Method for Prayer* (an updated version of a prayer originally published in 1710):

> Lord, give us grace to deny ourselves, to take up our cross daily,
>   and to follow Christ;
> to discipline our bodies and keep them under control.
>
> Lord, keep us from being lovers of ourselves,
> from being wise in our own eyes and leaning to our own
>   understanding.
>
> Lord, give us to seek, not our own good only, but also the good
>   of our neighbour.
>
> And grant that we may not live to ourselves or die to ourselves,
> but whether we live or die, we may be the Lord's,
> and may live and die to him. Amen.

● FURTHER STUDY

Here are two very different classics that are helpful in exploring the theme of this section more fully:

J. I. Packer, *A Passion for Holiness* (Crossway, 1992) is a rich and broad devotional exposition of the classic understanding of the way to holiness which gives greater attention to the place of the cross and the denial of self than is found in many more recent books on spirituality.

Richard Foster, *Celebration of Discipline* (Hodder & Stoughton, 1978) not only provides an excellent introduction to a range of spiritual disciplines, but is particularly helpful in its chapter on the discipline of simplicity, which relates closely to one aspect of the theme of self-denial.

Transformed: becoming like God's Son **in anticipation**

▶ GETTING STARTED

The heart of the early church pulsated at the thought that Jesus would soon return. The Christian story was far from over, and would be completed only when the Saviour whose crucifixion, resurrection and ascension they had witnessed reappeared. When he did so, the final act would be set in motion. Evil would be banished, judgment executed, truth vindicated and creation healed. God would have taken up his rightful place in his creation, and his rule over all would be unchallenged. Of particular relevance to us in these studies is that Christ's Second Coming will also mean that believers are transformed to live permanently in the presence of God and at long last be fully like Jesus.

As contemporary believers have been caught up with the problems of the present age, they have tended to conveniently ignore this aspect of the Christian gospel. But without it, the gospel is no real gospel at all. The return of Jesus provides us with hope for our broken world, and a great incentive for us as individuals to persevere in becoming like him.

While we should 'make every effort', as Peter exhorts us (2 Peter 1:5, 10; 3:14), to be as Christlike as possible in this life, we know that we'll never reach perfection here. That will happen only when Jesus returns.

READ *1 John 2:28 - 3:3*

And now, dear children, continue in him, so that when he appears we may be confident and unashamed before him at his coming.

If you know that he is righteous, you know that everyone who does what is right has been born of him.

See what great love the Father has lavished on us, that we should be called children of God! And that is what we are! The reason the world does not know us is that it did not know him. Dear friends, now we are children of God, and what we will be has not yet been made known. But we know that when Christ appears, we shall be like him, for we shall see him as he is. All who have this hope in him purify themselves, just as he is pure.

 FOCUS ON THE THEME

1. What place does the Second Coming of Jesus have in your thinking and your church's teaching?

 WHAT DOES THE BIBLE SAY?

2. On what grounds can we be 'confident and unashamed . . . at his coming' (2:28; 3:3)? If you dig around in 1 John 2:18 – 3:18, you will find several suggestions.

3. How does John reassure fearful Christians without encouraging spiritual complacency or over-confidence (3:1–2)?

4. What do you think John means when he writes, 'we shall be like him, for we shall see him as he is' (1 John 3:2)?

◎ GOING DEEPER

5. Sketch out the differences between our vision of Jesus now and the vision we will have of him when he returns.

6. What do the following texts teach us about being a 'work in progress'?
   - 2 Corinthians 3:18

   - Philippians 1:6

   - Philippians 3:12–14

7. How does 2 Peter 3:11–14 expand on John's brief call to purity in the light of the Second Coming?

Writing about love, Tom Wright explains,

It is the language Jesus spoke, and we are called to speak it so we can converse with him. It is the food they eat in God's new world, and we must acquire a taste for it here and now. It is the music God has written for all his creatures to sing, and we are called to learn it and practise it now so as to be ready when the conductor brings down his baton.

(Tom Wright, *Surprised by Hope*, p. 301)

 **LIVING IT OUT**

8. According to 1 John 3:1–2, how should I respond to the wobbles of the Christian life when doubts, failures or uncertainties arise?

9. In what respects can I still work at purifying my life?

10. Broadening the question beyond personal holiness, how does the picture of the new creation, set out in Revelation 21:1–8, inspire us to live now both as church members and as citizens?

▲ PRAYER TIME

Amen. Come, Lord Jesus.
(Revelation 22:20)

⬤ FURTHER STUDY

The following titles will help you think about our hope for the future:

Tom Wright, *Surprised by Hope* (SPCK, 2007)

J. Richard Middleton, *A New Heaven and a New Earth* (Baker, 2014)

Afterword

Paul wrote to the Galatians, 'My dear children, for whom I am again in the pains of childbirth until Christ is formed in you . . .' (4:19).

These few words are packed with meaning. They speak of Paul's pastoral passion and priority to see the church conforming to Christ in its belief and practice, visibly displaying Christ to the world. Any lesser goal (like keeping the church happy, or even keeping it open) is unworthy and short-changes the church. The words are realistic, indicating that achieving that goal is no easy task, but is as painful as giving birth. In the Galatians' case, what is holding them back from achieving the goal is that they have not fully understood the gospel of grace, and are still living by a doctrine of works. Other churches faced different hindrances on the path to Christ being formed in them.

Above all, the verse suggests that Christlikeness is more than an individual quest. It is a congregational goal and one that can be achieved only when we walk together in obedience to Christ. This needs stressing all the more in our present-day culture of individualism. As Michael Griffiths confessed some time ago,

I suddenly realize that there is a goal of congregational development and progress, which I may have been almost entirely overlooking. I had thought of the church primarily as something that will sometimes be of help to me. Now I began to realize that I have tremendous responsibilities to the congregation, because all of us are supposed to be developing and progressing together as a wonderful new community of God's people.

(Michael Griffiths, *Cinderella with Amnesia*, p. 31)

Don't fear that the path to becoming like Jesus is one we have to pursue on our own. God has designed that we should travel that path together.

Notes for leaders

SESSION 1

Godliness

1. This warm-up question should need no further explanation. Most people are only too happy to talk about how they find themselves becoming like their parents, like it or not, or how they see themselves reflected in their children.

2. The image of the vine stresses the organic nature of our union with Christ. We're not connected to him as we might join together Lego bricks or flat-pack furniture. The image highlights the living nature of our relationship, and Jesus as the indispensable source of our life and fruitfulness.

3. Jesus mentions two factors that contribute to our remaining in him. The first is obedience – keeping his words or commands (verses 7, 9, 10, 17) – and the second is remaining in his love (verse 9). We often view obedience as 'duty' and in tension with love. But they are never opposed in Jesus' mind. Obedience arises from love and makes love stronger. Love is never sentimental or cheap grace, but always leads to obedience. It is worth asking the group what it is that undermines their sense of God's ongoing love for them. Notice whether the lack of living in conformity with God's Word is mentioned.

4. Verse 8 says that bearing much fruit is the way to demonstrate that we are disciples of Jesus. The question to explore here is whether it is possible to be a genuine disciple if we are fruitless and unproductive. The purpose of our remaining in Christ is not so that we can enjoy a cosy relationship with him, but rather that we can be as useful to him as possible.

    The 'Further studies' section sheds more light on what kind of fruit Jesus has in mind.

5. Pruning may take many forms, but often comes in the guise of some adversity or other. Most of the great Bible characters experienced suffering, such as hardship or periods when God seemed to have

forgotten them, before they became fruitful leaders: think of Jacob wrestling with God after so long away from his family, Joseph in prison, Moses tending sheep in the wilderness, David as a fugitive, and so on. Frequently, gifted people need to be humbled and remodelled by God before they can become fruit-bearers.

Occasionally pruning takes the form of God removing a ministry from us that has become too important to us, and therefore an idol supplanting the place in our affections that belongs to God alone. Such pruning can be very painful indeed, especially as such ministries often provide us with our very identity.

According to Hebrews 12:4–13 such experiences are a sign of God's love.

6. Given the background mentioned in the 'Further studies' section, verse 6 primarily applies to Israel, rather than to individual believers today. It is a picture that Paul develops in his own way in Romans 11:11–24 about the future of Israel. While present-day believers in Christ have reason for assurance about their salvation, this verse suggests that, even so, no one can afford to be complacent. Hebrews 12:4–12 speaks of this using a different illustration.

7. On several occasions John patterns our relationship with Jesus on that of Christ's relationship with his Father. John stresses Jesus' intimate relationship with the Father (5:18), the way in which they honour each other (verse 23), the commission Jesus received from his Father (verse 27) and Jesus' total dependence on his Father (verse 30).

8. This question affords the opportunity of being practical. In addition to sharing experiences of Bible study and memorization, the group leader may like to have a number of resources available which encourage people to read God's Word regularly, profitably and with understanding.

9. This may be an opportunity for personal reflection as well as group discussion. If further guidance is needed, we might encourage the group to compare their prayers to that of, say, Nehemiah 1:4–11,

or Paul's prayers for the church (see Ephesians 3:14–21; Philippians 1:9–11; Colossians 1:9–14).

10. The sad truth is that very few churches are making disciples today, and very few Christians are effective in leading others to Christ. Perhaps that is not the only measure of what it means to bear fruit, but it is one important measure nonetheless. The leader should discourage the group from degenerating into a moaning session or simply 'church bashing'. Channel the discussion in a positive direction, asking how we can become more intentional in producing fruit.

Character

1. Try to move past comments like 'they're nice people', and be more specific about qualities that are attractive or unattractive. Equally, try to move past 'middle-class niceness' by relating the characteristics mentioned to those listed in the passage under consideration here.

2. According to verses 1–4, the positive secret of Christlikeness is determinedly to focus our hearts and minds on Christ. It requires that we refuse to be dictated to by the earthly culture around us, and rise above it as we fix our eyes on Jesus and adopt his priorities. It matters, because the very essence of the Christian life is to be united to Christ who is risen and exalted in heaven.

   Negatively, it involves putting our earthly nature to death (verse 5). Just as the crucifixion is central to our salvation, so it is central to our Christian experience. It is not only that Christ died for us, but also that we died with him (Romans 6:3). The New Testament speaks of this from several angles: 'I have been crucified with Christ' (Galatians 2:20); 'Those who belong to Christ Jesus have crucified the flesh with its passions and desires' (Galatians 5:24); 'the world has been crucified to me' (Galatians 6:14); 'becoming like him in his death' (Philippians 3:10).

   Crucifixion was both a decisive, irreversible event and also a process of lingering death, with some victims taking days to die. So this calls Christians to a decisive, irreversible commitment not to live according to our pre-Christ lives and also to renew daily our resolve to put to death the old way of life.

3. Our culture is very individualistic, unlike in New Testament times. So issues of character were never just about personal qualities, but were inevitably also about relationships. Verse 11 speaks of this explicitly, but the other virtues mentioned in verses 12–14 were relational qualities, and it is impossible to put verses 15–17 into practice in a social vacuum.

4. Two tools are mentioned to help our progress in character transformation: the Word and worship. The 'message of Christ' is to be deeply imbibed rather than occasionally sipped. And we're to do this individually and with 'one another'. When instructing each other, we must take care not to let unwise enthusiasm get the better of us. Wisdom is needed. Worship is also vital: worship that can provide us with a balanced, all-round experience of prayer, praise and instruction, not worship that is partisan or stuck in one particular cultural rut. After all, the church of God is composed of all types (verse 11), and our worship should mirror that harmony we find in Christ.

5. The Colossian Christians lived in fear of malicious powers and authorities (see 1:17; 2:15). They lacked the confidence that Christ was the sole, sufficient and supreme power who could deliver them and defeat their enemies (see 1:15–20; 2:6–15). So they tried to supplement the gospel of Jesus, as 2:16–23 shows, with other religious beliefs and experiences to make sure they were safe. In seeking to build their confidence in Christ, Paul stresses not what will happen to them in the future, but what has already happened to them if they have trusted in the risen and exalted Christ alone.

6. People are keen on 'designer labels' these days. But what is the 'designer wardrobe' that a Christian is to wear? If it helps to think concretely, go through your wardrobe relating various garments to the virtues we should all wear.

7. Jesus Christ is the one human being in whom the image of God was perfectly displayed, without in any way being marred by sin. Meditate on the human Christ and the qualities he showed, and give attention to how they may impact the way we live.

8. Dividing our lives into the spiritual and the secular, church (which is where things really count) and the rest (like a job we do merely to pay the bills) is a false, even fatal, division. Jesus is Lord over the whole of our lives – work, family and leisure, as much as our church activities. John Bunyan described Mr Talkative as 'a saint abroad and a devil at

home' – not someone to copy! Christlikeness needs to permeate every aspect of our lives.

9. Racism is a sin, and churches that harbour racist attitudes are living contrary to God's Word. In a multiracial context it's not difficult to enjoy genuine, deep and wonderfully enriching Christian fellowship with those across ethnic divides. Let the group share their experiences of doing so. Discuss some of the practical cultural issues that get in the way, and imagine what steps can be taken to portray Christ's multiracial new community more accurately.

10. Gratitude is a healthy spiritual discipline, and its absence leads to negativism, self-pity and grumbling. A lack of gratitude also results in our building barriers to good relations with others. Before asking God for anything fresh, encourage the group to stop and thank him for all they have received already.

SESSION 3

Serving

1. One of the themes of *Downton Abbey* was the struggle of the privileged classes to adapt to a changing world that was less aristocratic and more democratic. The world of *Downton* may have passed, but the division between the powerful and the poor, the rulers and the servants, remains. Update the picture, by all means, but try to encourage the group to reflect honestly on where they are, or where they'd like to be, in the contemporary social pyramid.

2. John emphasizes that although Jesus knew that within hours he would be taken into custody, interrogated, humiliated, flogged and crucified (verse 1), he still focuses on his disciples and engages in this extraordinary act of service. What does this say to us in a culture that often encourages people to be preoccupied with their own issues and problems?

3. Washing the feet of guests was the task of a low-ranking servant, not the host. Peers didn't wash each other's feet. Some Jews even thought that only Gentile slaves should undertake this task, since it was too menial a duty for a fellow-Jew. So 'his act of humility is as unnecessary as it is stunning' (D. A. Carson, *The Gospel According to John*, p. 462).

4. Verses 12–17 give several reasons why we should wash one another's feet: (a) to obey our Master; (b) to follow his example; (c) to indicate that we know our place; and (d) to receive God's blessing on our lives.

5. Almost every line of Isaiah 42:1–4 applies to Jesus. God's choice, delight and Spirit-empowerment were evident at Jesus' baptism. His gentleness towards those damaged by life was evident in his actions and miracles. He demonstrated a clear commitment to truth and justice and bringing hope throughout his life, especially by challenging the authorities of his day. And he did not give in to discouragement, or give up, even in the face of outright opposition, betrayal and death. Instead, he loved his own 'to the end' (John 13:1).

6. John Stott suggests that John 13 is a dramatic enactment of the hymn in Philippians 2, and he draws several parallels between them. He '"got up from the meal" as he had risen from his throne'. He took off his outer garments, as he laid aside his glory. He wrapped a towel around his waist, as he took on the nature of a servant. He poured water into a basin, as he was to pour out his life in death. When he had finished, 'he put on his clothes and returned to his place. After the humiliation of the cross he returned clothed in exaltation to his Father' (John Stott, *The Incomparable Christ*, p. 144).

7. Jesus washed his disciples' feet as their 'Teacher' and 'Lord'. In doing so, he demonstrated the true nature of Christian leadership. It is all about serving, from beginning to end. James and John found it hard to think in those counter-cultural terms and still saw it as a matter of status and power in their conversation with Jesus in Mark 10:35–45. How do you think Christian leadership measures up (or should it be down?) to this idea today?

8. This question involves an exercise in self-awareness. Do we read ourselves aright, or do we think we're humble servants when others see us as arrogant and waiting to be served? If you know and trust each other well in the group, maybe you can do this together. But it may be better done more privately.

9. Some churches practise ceremonial foot washing (often on Maundy Thursday), and testify to how moving it is. But by repeating the ceremony, are we in danger of missing the point? In Jesus' day people walked without socks and wore open sandals, so foot washing was necessary. But that doesn't usually happen today! Discuss a variety of contemporary equivalents and what anyone is doing about them.

10. Avoid this degenerating into a leader-bashing session. Leadership is tough, and leaders have to respond to a multitude of often conflicting expectations. But in what realistic ways could the style of leadership become more servant-like and less lordly?

SESSION 4

Compassion

1. Most of us bump into charity collectors on the street, and are inundated with unsolicited mail or cold calls seeking a donation towards a worthy cause. How do the group deal with this? Do people respond to some and not others, and if so, on what basis? Do some restrict their giving to appeals through the church or from known Christian organizations whose reputation can be trusted? What are the strengths and weaknesses of giving only to Christian appeals?

2. The longed-for rest, which Jesus and his disciples deserved, was denied them, as the crowd walked the ten miles around the lake to find them. Ordinary people might have reacted with resentment that their private space had been invaded, but Jesus was deeply moved by their leaderless quest for direction. Does he serve as a model for us to emulate? The disciples seem less patient and overwhelmed by practical questions, which may be a more normal human reaction. But is it the right one?

3. There are two aspects to this question. One concerns the image of a flock of sheep without a shepherd, first mentioned by Moses in Numbers 27:16–17. Shepherdless sheep would soon be in trouble, since they would lack food, not be able to find their way to good pasture and be without protection from danger. It was an apt description for the children of Israel.

   The second concerns the size of the crowd. When a problem is daunting to us, it is not so with God, who created the world from nothing and still sustains and resources his creation. Reference might be made to Luke 17:11–19 where Jesus heals ten men with leprosy, his largest single act of healing. Note, he has mercy on them and moves to heal their physical condition, irrespective of whether they are Jews or Samaritans, or of whether or not they are going to thank God for it. This has much to teach us about the breadth of Jesus' compassion.

4. The feeding of the 5,000 supremely tells us that God cares about people. The story echoes God's feeding of Israel in the wilderness (Exodus 16) and demonstrates God's concern for the whole person – body and soul. It teaches us that Jesus is his Father's Son.

5. Note the word 'So' in verse 34. Jesus' compassion led him to prioritize teaching over feeding. As Jesus reminded Satan, 'Man shall not live on bread alone, but on every word that comes from the mouth of God' (Matthew 4:4). Teaching someone to live in the light of God's Word is the most compassionate thing we can do. Without it, compassionate acts may sometimes prove to be a mere sticking plaster over someone's problems and never enable them to live differently, free from what caused the problem in the first place. This will not always be the case, since sometimes people are victims of circumstances for which they are not personally responsible. Even so, compassionate intervention can be used as an opportunity to teach truth about our merciful God.

   Jesus' prioritizing of teaching provokes us to ask whether the contemporary church has lost this vision and replaced it merely with compassionate social actions.

6. In Matthew 19 Jesus acts compassionately when he confronts physical and spiritual sickness, social ostracism, death and disability.

   Compassion is never a one-size-fits-all exercise, but rather a response to people's particular needs. In these verses Jesus responds by inspiring his disciples to join in reaping the harvest, healing the sick, giving sight to the blind and including those who had been blind, and therefore isolated from others, in his band of disciples.

7. From the beginning God revealed himself to be a God of compassion. Exodus 34:6 is repeated in some form in 2 Chronicles 30:9; Nehemiah 9:17; Joel 2:13; Jonah 4:2; Nahum 1:3; and five times in the Psalms. His compassion is not in conflict with his holiness and justice, since compassion requires that evil is confronted and sin is punished. And God has dealt with this for us in his Son Jesus Christ. There are not two Gods in the Bible – an Old Testament God of wrath and a New Testament God of grace – but only one.

8. Because the world's problems are so great and we cannot solve them all, many feel that it's not worthwhile doing anything. 'It makes so little difference,' we hear people say. True, but remember the old story of a person picking up fish that were struggling for survival on a beach and throwing them back into the water. 'Why bother?' shrugged a passer-by. 'The number of fish is so enormous that you'll never be able to save them all.' 'No,' the reply came, 'but I'll make a difference to the ones I can.'

9. Whether deserved or not, the reputation of the church is often one of hypocrisy and cold respectability which exudes disapproval. Mark Twain commented on people who are 'good in the worst sense of the word'. Sustained and practical compassionate action is needed in order to overturn this image. Why not gather some stories about where this has happened and where the church enjoys 'the favour of all the people' (Acts 2:47)?

10. The Old Testament law of the tithe is neither explicitly taught nor explicitly withdrawn in the New Testament. A better guide to giving under the new covenant is set out in 1 Corinthians 16:1–2 and 2 Corinthians 8 – 9, and especially in 9:6–9.

Justice

1. Luke uses a variety of terms to talk about those who were, at best, on the margins of society in Jesus' day. Their situation may have been caused by their job (for example, tax collectors who were working for an occupying power), their health (those who were unclean because of leprosy or other disease) or their situation (the widowed or those in dire straits for other reasons). This question aims to get the discussion going by considering who might fit some of those descriptions today.

2. The source of Jesus' power was the anointing of the Holy Spirit. The Spirit 'descended on him' at his baptism (Luke 3:22), when God commissioned him at the start of his public ministry. Kings and prophets were commissioned for their roles by anointing. Supremely, the Messiah was the Anointed One.

   Like Jesus, we need the anointing of the Holy Spirit for our mission, or we will become merely another group of social or political activists. The Spirit both directs us into particular work and empowers us for it. His role is constantly to shed the spotlight on Jesus and bring his teaching alive to us. As such, Jesus becomes the focus of all Spirit-empowered mission.

3. There are two elements to this question. First, it asks us to consider the meaning of the word 'proclaim', which appears twice in verse 18. We often use this word in the limited sense of verbal proclamation or, even more specifically, preaching. But proclamation is wider than this and may take place through signs and demonstrations of kingdom power as well as in speech. Even so, actions always need interpretation.

   Second, the question invites us to consider the meaning of the word 'gospel' or 'good news'. Contemporary evangelicalism often reduces the gospel to a slick formula, but the Gospels themselves, as well as the New Testament generally, reveal it to be a multifaceted message of good news, expressed and experienced in a variety of ways, although its core is always about salvation and reconciliation with God through the cross and resurrection.

4. Many take these words merely as a template for social action today. But when Jesus spoke them, he did so not primarily to provide us with a pattern for our action, but to claim that he was the fulfilment of Isaiah's prophecy and that the new age of 'the Lord's favour' was being initiated by him, through his life, death and resurrection. To speak of mission while ignoring the essential place of Christ in this manifesto is to be content with the husk rather than the kernel of the wheat.

5. Some take these words very literally to refer, for example, to those in economic poverty. Yet, while these verses may embrace a literal meaning, they are probably capable of a wider interpretation and can apply to any who are marginalized or oppressed by 'respectable' society. When first recorded in Isaiah 66:1–2, they were a vision of Israel's release from the exile in Babylon and their restoration to an abundant and prosperous homeland.

6. Isaiah 61:2 continues, 'and the day of vengeance of our God'. It is often said that Jesus omitted these words because his mission was one of salvation, and not, at that time, one of judgment. John 3:17 sheds some light on this, and John 5:22–30 shows that Jesus will act as judge, but that was not the purpose of his mission on earth. This point seems to be underlined when Jesus immediately proceeds to refer to two non-Israelite examples – the widow in Zarephath and Naaman the Syrian – as examples of God's inclusive grace (Luke 4:24–30).

    The slight reservation about this view is that Jesus also omits the phrase 'to comfort all who mourn' from the Isaiah passage, although his ministry was self-evidently one of comforting the mournful.

7. The Jubilee Year of Leviticus 25:8–55 occurred every fiftieth year (after seven Sabbath years). It began with the blowing of a trumpet and the proclamation of liberty for any who had fallen into debt, enabling them to return to their property. This way of releasing fellow Israelites from debt slavery was a last resort, which would come into play only if previous steps to solve the problem had failed. It was a way of

preventing the rich from endlessly amassing wealth at the expense of the poor who might otherwise have been forever caught in the poverty trap. It reflected the horror that the Israelites always felt towards slavery after their experience in Egypt.

Scholars dispute whether these radical economics were ever practised in Israel, but the evidence suggests that they were not. Until, that is, the coming of Jesus. Many see Jesus' ministry as 'proclaiming liberty throughout the land' (Leviticus 25:10) through his releasing of those who were in slavery to debt, demons, sickness and social injustice, as fulfilling the vision of the Jubilee year.

8. This might be a place for testimony, as there are some wonderful stories of the oppressed being set free today. But if people cannot speak from personal experience, make sure that there are some stories to hand from other churches or missionary agencies which will encourage confidence in the liberating power of the gospel.

9. Contemporary mission that claims to be holistic or integrated often proves in practice to be 'Jesus-lite', and concerned about social action almost to the exclusion of the evangelistic message. Remember, Luke's radical social commitment regularly connects Jesus' liberating actions with the forgiveness of sins. See Luke 5:17–26; 7:36–48; 24:45–48.

10. Not all churches relate to their communities easily, since in some cases members travel from a distance in order to attend. Even if it is located within a residential area, a church sometimes has an ill-informed, impressionistic view of a community's needs. Rather than keeping established patterns of churchgoing, maybe greater community knowledge could suggest new or different avenues of mission. For example, one church was determined to keep their Sunday school open, although there were few families living nearby and there was an urgent need for an older persons' lunch club. Once they woke up to this fact, it transformed their outreach and mission. Encourage the group to contact local agencies and professionals to find out about the community's real needs.

Suffering

1. Many of us automatically equate suffering with physical illness. But keep a broad view of suffering in mind, since it may take the form of persecution, injustice, false accusation, circumstantial misfortune, natural disaster or a host of other adversities. It's worth injecting James 1:2–4 into the conversation here.

2. While the idea of redemptive suffering was familiar to the Jewish people in Jesus' day, as Isaiah 53 illustrates, the idea of the Messiah suffering was contrary to all expectations. Peter had just declared Jesus to be the Messiah (Mark 8:29), and the thought of his being killed didn't fit the picture. The Messiah was expected to be a royal figure, like King David, only greater, who would free Israel from their enemies by military victory, not by apparent failure. Crucifixion – a form of execution meted out on the defeated riff-raff of the Roman world – was incompatible with the hopes they had of Jesus as the Messiah.

3. When circumstances are imposed on us, we often speak of 'having to bear our cross'. Or we joke (or used to) about our mothers-in-law as the 'cross we have to bear'! But Jesus' teaching here is a little different. It's not about putting up with things we can't help, but deliberately embracing a cross we could avoid.

    What did he mean? He identifies taking up the cross with denying oneself (verse 34) and losing one's life (verse 35). Note the purpose of losing one's life is 'for me and for the gospel'. Bearing the cross is not about enhancing one's own life, but about furthering the mission of Jesus and for the glory of God.

4. The temptation here is to tell glowing stories of missionaries who have risked, or even lost, their lives for the gospel. But Jesus' challenge is for all disciples, not just an elite. Think of more ordinary examples, closer to home, which may inspire the group. I think, for example, of a couple who served as foster parents for many children down the

years, losing the privacy and comfort, and sometimes even the stability, of their own home, and foregoing the potential of earning greater incomes, for the sake of needy children. Others have dedicated themselves to youth work, with no thought of their own needs.

5. The use of the word 'must' witnesses to the divine necessity of Christ's suffering and death. It was the means God devised for our salvation, and without it salvation would not have been accomplished. Isaiah 53:10–11 gives some insight into the background to this. Care must be taken not to imply that an angry God imposed abuse on an unwilling Son. Jesus fully and voluntarily embraced the cross, as Hebrews 10:5–10 explains. 'Must' speaks of the constraints of grace that led Father and Son on the path to the cross.

6. This question should be placed in the wider context of verses 27–30. Peter had just openly confessed the breakthrough insight that Jesus was the Messiah and, according to Matthew's account, he had been called 'blessed' by Jesus and appointed to be the rock of the church (see Matthew 16:17). Now suddenly he is subject to the harshest of rebukes. It is an outstanding lesson in our human vulnerability, especially when we have just enjoyed a special spiritual blessing.

   Satan is always an accuser and always looking for a person through whom he can accomplish his destructive goals. He 'prowls around like a roaring lion looking for someone to devour' (1 Peter 5:8). On this occasion his victim was Peter, who thought he could correct Jesus and persuade him to sidestep the cross. But in doing so, Peter revealed how much he was thinking in terms of conventional wisdom, rather than in the upside-down logic of God's kingdom.

7. The heart of our Christian experience is 'union with Christ'. One way or another, being 'in Christ' is mentioned over 130 times in Paul's letters. The only Christ with whom we can be united is the crucified Christ, and so to be united to him necessarily involves our embracing his cross for ourselves. There is no way to avoid the cross in our quest to become like Jesus.

8. The contrast with conventional culture, with its need to 'get ahead' and its 'look after oneself' mentality, should be obvious. But its influence is subtle and runs so deep within us that we may not always recognize it. Hence, we need to talk together about such matters, and it may even be helpful to have a Christian from another culture to reflect with us on our lifestyles.

    The secret here will be to direct the group to address the question of how we can encourage each other positively to a Jesus mindset, rather than allow the study to become a moaning session about contemporary life.

9. Few who were crucified in the Roman world were executed in this way as a matter of personal choice! True, their crucifixion may have been the consequence of their earlier lifestyle choices, such as opposing Rome or committing crime. But none would have chosen death by this most barbaric and degrading form of execution. Yet Jesus calls his disciples to make such a conscious choice.

    Discuss whether there are spiritual disciplines of self-denial one can adopt so that we might not lose our souls. Traditionally, spiritual disciplines have involved fasting from food. That's still relevant in an obese-prone culture, although the reason for fasting is for the sake of one's spiritual rather than physical health. But is fasting a broader concept? In our material world should we learn to forego what others take for granted? Should we deny ourselves, for example, the right to leisure, luxury material possessions, personal comfort, social media? What other 'self-denials' might the group suggest?

10. Too often the lifestyle values of the church are indistinguishable from those found in nice middle-class suburbia. Christians may be as selfishly ambitious – for their children, if not for themselves – or as comfort-seeking as their non-Christian neighbours. Radicalism is often something taught to our young people, in the hope that they'll grow out of it later on.

    What steps can we take to keep the radical teaching and mindset of Jesus constantly before us? One simple way may be to encourage each other to undermine the pressure of the advertisers who suggest that we're left behind if we don't buy this or have that. Some years ago a bishop encouraged Christians to shout 'Enough is enough' at the TV when adverts appeared. Perhaps it's worth reviving the shout!

SESSION 7

Anticipation

1. The teaching about Jesus' return is largely unheard today. Few preach it, and basic introductions to the Christian faith often omit it, although it was part of the core of apostolic teaching. Several reasons might be suggested for this. Perhaps 'this world' seems all too real so that we can't see beyond it. Perhaps unwise interpretations and overexcited views in the twentieth century led to the doctrine as a whole being discredited. As we have become more comfortable in this life, the thought that 'This world is not my home. I'm just a-passing through' has faded, and we've settled here. And other-worldly preaching seems to have little to say to the real struggles that the world is facing on a global scale.

    Perhaps the group can suggest other reasons why the doctrine of the Second Coming has been muted and how it might be presented credibly in the present day.

2. The first letter of John sets out several ways in which we can be confident in the light of the Second Coming, including that we continue in the faith that Jesus is the Christ, and are not led astray by false teaching (2:18–27), that we live pure sin-free lives in so far as it is possible to do so (3:3–6), and that we love in very practical and tangible ways (3:16–18). This, rather than having some mystical experiences, is what it means to 'continue in him' (2:28).

3. John proves to be a superb pastor. Through this letter he provides apprehensive believers with solid grounds for assurance. This reaches its climax here in the ringing declaration in 3:1–2 that we are already children of God. Note the emphasis on 'now' in verse 2. Yet he balances this with recognition that we have not fully entered into our salvation or been fully transformed into Christlikeness. So there are no grounds for presuming that we have arrived. The Christian life is lived in the constant tension of the 'now' and the 'not yet'.

4. There are several passages that contrast our current vision of Jesus with the ultimate vision we will have. Currently we 'see only a reflection as in a mirror' and only 'know in part' (1 Corinthians 13:12). Similarly, at present we 'live by faith, not by sight' (2 Corinthians 5:7). It's the difference between knowing a person from a distance, by letter or social media, and being with them. The former may be good as far as it goes, and not in any way misleading. But there is no substitute for actually being with someone – to know them and be known by them fully. Only when we encounter him fully will ultimate transformation into his likeness occur.

5. Our vision of Jesus will no longer consist of occasional glimpses, but will be permanent. It will no longer be obscured by our sinful disobedience, or by our sufferings on earth. We will see him as he truly is, the risen and exalted Lord, the overlord of all creation, the Lamb, once slain but now standing as a Lion in heaven. We will experience directly the reality of John's vision of Christ in Revelation 1:12–16. We will see so much more, including the intimate relationship between Father and Son with our eyes, rather than just hearing of it from Jesus' lips.

6. All of these texts speak of the Christian life as one of progressive growth into Christlikeness. In 2 Corinthians 3:18 it says that we 'are being transformed', Philippians 1:6 indicates that the task won't be complete 'until the day of Christ Jesus', and in Philippians 3:12 Paul states that he has not arrived at his goal, but is pressing on. These verses speak of continuous progress being made in this life. Neither here, nor elsewhere in the New Testament, is any encouragement given to the idea that we can achieve perfection or reach our complete spiritual destination in this life. That is realized only on 'the day of Christ'.

   Note how, when placed alongside each other, these verses testify to our progressive transformation as both a work of God and his Spirit, and a result of human commitment and perseverance. Two prime texts that teach this are Philippians 2:12–13 ('continue to work out your salvation . . . for it is God who works in you') and

2 Peter 1:3–5 ('His divine power has given us everything we need for a godly life . . . For this very reason, make every effort to add to your faith goodness . . .').

7. The second letter of Peter is written in a context of scepticism regarding the return of Christ, and, unlike John, Peter writes about his coming in apocalyptic terms. But his call to let our future destination in the new heaven and new earth govern the way we live on earth now is the same as John's. We should get in training: living already as we will be living then. John mentions the need for purity. Peter expands the thought using a variety of terms. He speaks of the need for 'holy and godly lives', 'righteousness', and of being 'spotless, blameless and at peace with him' (3:11–14).

8. In his first letter John is very conscious that some believers are insecure in their relationship with God, and he sets out to provide assurance. Here the basis of our assurance is that we are already children of God. There may be days when a child doesn't feel as if they are their parents' son or daughter, but nothing can alter the facts. Human families, of course, are far from perfect, and parents may send out signals that their children are unwanted, by neglecting, abusing or rejecting them. But it's not so with God. John 1:11–12 provides some background here. In the end, the relationship doesn't depend on feelings, but on facts.

    We return to the question of insecurity in 1 John 3:19–20. This time John says that when we hear the voice of self-accusation in our lives, there is a greater voice to which we should pay attention: the voice of God. His is the one that counts, and his is the voice of grace. We need not fear that God would reject us if he knew a little more about us, or found us out in some way, since already 'he knows everything' and still welcomes us into his family.

9. We often associate purity with the sexual dimension of our lives, and rightly so. Yet the Bible has a much broader vision of purity. Galatians 5:19–21, Ephesians 4:25–27 and Colossians 3:5–9 all list a range of impurities from which we should cleanse our lives, including anger, undisciplined emotions, selfishness, gossip, resentment, greed, lack

of integrity, foul language, lying, ingratitude and divisiveness. Is the church constantly in danger of restricting its understanding of purity?

10. If you want to get physically fit, you join a gym or undergo a training regime. This is an opportunity to discuss what might be the spiritual equivalent.

Books mentioned in the text

D. A. Carson, *The Gospel According to John*, Pillar New Testament Commentaries (IVP, 1991)

Tim Chester, 'Walk Humbly with Your God', in Marijke Hoek and Justin Thacker (eds.), *Micah's Challenge: The Church's Responsibility for the Global Poor* (Paternoster, 2008)

Gordon D. Fee, *Paul's Letter to the Philippians*, New International Commentary on the New Testament (Eerdmans, 1995)

Richard Foster, *Celebration of Discipline* (Hodder & Stoughton, 1978)

R. T. France, *The Gospel of Matthew*, New International Commentary on the New Testament (Eerdmans, 2007)

Timothy George, *Galatians*, The New American Commentary (Broadman & Holman, 1994)

Michael Griffiths, *Cinderella with Amnesia: A Practical Discussion of the Relevance of the Church* (IVP, 1975)

Marijke Hoek and Justin Thacker (eds.), *Micah's Challenge: The Church's Responsibility for the Global Poor* (Paternoster, 2008)

J. Richard Middleton, *A New Heaven and a New Earth* (Baker, 2014)

Bruce Milne, *The Message of John*, The Bible Speaks Today (IVP, 1993)

J. I Packer, *A Passion for Holiness* (Crossway, 1992)

C. René Padilla, 'The Kingdom of God and the Mission of the Church', in Marijke Hoek and Justin Thacker (eds.), *Micah's Challenge: The Church's Responsibility for the Global Poor* (Paternoster, 2008)

John Stott, *The Incomparable Christ* (IVP, 2001)

William Temple, *Readings in St John's Gospel* (many editions; first published by MacMillan, 1939)

Jim Wallis, *On God's Side* (Brazos Press, 2013)

Warren W. Wiersbe, *The Best of A. W. Tozer* (Crossway, 1978)

Tom Wright, *Surprised by Hope* (SPCK, 2007)

About Keswick Ministries

Our purpose

Keswick Ministries is committed to the spiritual renewal of God's people for his mission in the world.

God's purpose is to bring his blessing to all the nations of the world. That promise of blessing, which touches every aspect of human life, is ultimately fulfilled through the life, death, resurrection, ascension and future return of Christ. All of the people of God are called to participate in his missionary purposes, wherever he may place them. The central vision of Keswick Ministries is to see the people of God equipped, encouraged and refreshed to fulfil that calling, directed and guided by God's Word in the power of his Spirit, for the glory of his Son.

Our priorities

Keswick Ministries seeks to serve the local church through:

- **Hearing God's Word**: the Scriptures are the foundation for the church's life, growth and mission, and Keswick Ministries is committed to preach and teach God's Word in a way that is faithful to Scripture and relevant to Christians of all ages and backgrounds.

- **Becoming like God's Son**: from its earliest days the Keswick movement has encouraged Christians to live godly lives in the power of the Spirit, to grow in Christlikeness and to live under his lordship in every area of life. This is God's will for his people in every culture and generation.

- **Serving God's mission**: the authentic response to God's Word is obedience to his mission, and the inevitable result of Christlikeness is sacrificial service. Keswick Ministries seeks to encourage committed discipleship in family life, work and society, and energetic engagement in the cause of world mission.

Our ministry

- **Keswick: the event**. Every summer the town of Keswick hosts a three-week Convention, which attracts some 15,000 Christians from the UK and around the world. The event provides Bible teaching for all ages, vibrant worship, a sense of unity across generations and denominations, and an inspirational call to serve Christ in the world. It caters for children of all ages and has a strong youth and young adult programme. And it all takes place in the beautiful Lake District – a perfect setting for rest, recreation and refreshment.

- **Keswick: the movement**. For 140 years the work of Keswick has impacted churches worldwide, and today the movement is underway throughout the UK, as well as in many parts of Europe, Asia, North America, Australia, Africa and the Caribbean. Keswick Ministries is committed to strengthen the network in the UK and beyond, through prayer, news, pioneering and cooperative activity.

- **Keswick resources**. Keswick Ministries is producing a growing range of books and booklets based on the core foundations of Christian life and mission. It makes Bible teaching available through free access to mp3 downloads, and the sale of DVDs and CDs. It broadcasts online through Clayton TV and annual BBC Radio 4 services. In addition to the summer Convention, Keswick Ministries is hoping to develop other teaching and training events in the coming years.

Our unity

The Keswick movement worldwide has adopted a key Pauline statement to describe its gospel inclusivity: 'for you are all one in Christ Jesus' (Galatians 3:28). Keswick Ministries works with evangelicals from a wide variety of church backgrounds, on the understanding that they share a commitment to the essential truths of the Christian faith as set out in our statement of belief.

Our contact details
Mail: Keswick Ministries, Keswick Convention Centre, Skiddaw Street, Keswick, CA12 4BY England
T: 017687 80075
E: info@keswickministries.org
W: www: keswickministries.org